The Treasures Of Godly Wisdom

Christa Miller

The New King James Bible, New Testament
Copyright © 1979 by Thomas Nelson, Inc.

The New King James Bible, New Testament and Psalms
Copyright © 1980 by Thomas Nelson, Inc.

The Holy Bible, New King James Version
Copyright © 1982, by Thomas Nelson, Inc.

The New Student Bible, New International Version®
Copyright © 1973, 1978, 1984 by International Bible Society

"Scripture taken from the Holy Bible, New International Version, Copyright © 1973, 1978, 1984 International Bible Society, Used by Permission of Zondervan Publishing House."

Copyright © 2006   Christa Miller

All rights reserved. No part of this publication may be reproduced, stored in a retrieval system, or transmitted in any form or by any means, electronic, mechanical, photocopying, recording, or otherwise, without the prior written permission of the publisher.

ISBN: 1-933899-26-3

Published by:
Holy Fire Publishing
Unit 116
1525-D Old Trolley Rd.
Summerville, SC 29485
www.ChristianPublish.com

Cover Design: Jay Cookingham
Illustrations by: Stephanie Depro

Printed in the United States of America and the United Kingdom

Dedication

I thank God for all of my "cheerleaders" in BSF☺: Freida Cardwell, Debbie Fox, Brandi Greene, Vicki Hurley, Vivian Lee, Cherie Lukefahr, Jennifer Powers, Denise Ratcliff, Alison Staggs, Milissa Wheeler, and Nikki White. I thank God for all the support each of you have given to me. God has something good in store for each of you girls.

Many thanks to Stephanie Depro for doing the pictures. I'm so grateful you dedicated your time to do these. They are wonderful!

I also give many thanks and love to my parents, John and Judy Jones. Thank you for all of your prayers-see what all of that has done? I appreciate your faithfulness of raising me in a godly home. And Mom, *thanks a lot* for proofreading this. I love the both of you very much.

To my in-laws, Bob and Terry Casto: Your God-given encouragement, your love and guidance was greatly appreciated. I'm glad to be a part of your family. I love the both of you.

To my husband, BJ: I thank God for you and your incredible support you've given me this entire time of writing this book. I say this with lots of love and many years together I pray☺.

To my daughter, Annabeth: When you'll be able to read this, I just want you to know that you were and always will be special to me no matter what. You are a gift from God. And I pray you'll come to know Christ as I have known Him.

> *I wouldn't have been able to write this book without God. His faithfulness and His love have been so great. All things are possible with Him!*
> *(Mark 10:27)*

Table of Contents

1. Keeping your Spiritual House Clean — 7
2. Joyful Living — 17
3. The Glory of Steadfastness — 25
4. Love Made Complete — 43
5. Cast All Your Cares — 55
6. What the Cross can do for You — 65
7. Hearing God's Voice — 79

Keeping your Spiritual House Clean

II Corinthians 7:1
Since we have these promises, dear friends, let us purify ourselves from everything that contaminates body and spirit, perfecting holiness out of reverence for God.

This chapter helps you discover the ways that are purifying and rewarding when you let your everlasting Father live in your life. It gives discernment of things that prevents you from living for God.

Romans 5:21
Just as sin reigned in death, so also grace might reign through righteousness to bring eternal life through Jesus Christ our Lord.

Picture this house as your spiritual home inside you. How is yours built? Is your house built to withstand the storms of life?_____your name_____, come inside and see what Jesus has to give you.

Trust Jesus with *everything* in your life and you will find all the treasures He has for you. In Him, you will find shelter from life's stormy situations within your innermost being.

He's inviting you to have eternal life with Him. Trade all of your past mistakes and your pain all for the glory of the Lord and leave *all* of your past behind.

God's Goodness

Proverbs 3:5
Trust in the Lord with all your heart and lean not on your own understanding.

Why would you want to partake in *any* evil when Jesus is ultimately pure and holy?

When tempted to sin, God's power is more than the temptation itself. The temptation becomes weak when God's Word is spoken.

I Corinthians 10:13
No temptation has seized you except what is common to man. And God is faithful; He will not let you be tempted beyond what you can bear. But when you are tempted, He will also provide a way out so that you can stand up under it.

For God's glory in your life, purify yourselves from those things that contaminate your God-shaped hole.
These certain things may be unforgiveness, wrong motives, and negative words. By being obedient to Him, He will direct your paths.

I John 2:15-17
"Do not love the world or anything in the world. If anyone loves the world, the love of the Father is not in him. For everything in the world-the cravings of

sinful man, the lust of his eyes and the boasting of what he has and does-comes not from the Father but from the world. The world and its desires pass away, but the man who does the will of God lives forever."

God allows certain things to happen to perfect you.

Romans 8:28
And we know that in all things God works for the good of those who love Him, who have been called according to His purpose.

To start your day off right, seek God's word He has for you and follow His precepts.

Ecclesiastes 8:5
Whoever obeys His command will come to no harm and the wise heart will know the proper time and procedure.

Proverbs 4:22
For they are life to those who find them, and health to all their flesh.

God is Sovereign

John 10:9
I am the door. If anyone enters by Me, he will be saved.

Is there a lack of faith in God? God Almighty is in charge of cleaning out *all* the doubt Satan planted in your path.

Ephesians 1:18-19
I pray also that the eyes of your heart may be enlightened in order that you may know the hope to which He has called you, the riches of His glorious inheritance in the saints, and His incomparably great power for us who believe.

Be careful of what you allow in your life. What may seem to be innocent may do more harm than you think. For instance, choose friends who lift you up rather than ones that bring you down. Wait for God's best that He has for you.

Ecclesiastes 8:5a
Whoever obeys His command will come to no harm.

For those who do not have the things you need, just ask the Lord. His word says to ask, seek and knock and the door will be opened (Luke 11:9). All of your cares are in the palm of His hand and will be answered accordingly to His perfect will.

Ask, seek and knock to invite the Light of the World. Know in confidence that He'll answer your prayer.

Trust in God

Matthew 18:4
Therefore whoever humbles himself like this child is the greatest in the kingdom of heaven.

Is there pride in your home? You can identify it through the way you react or feel to certain situations. One thing I learned from pride is that it's not good; it doesn't lift you up higher. Forfeit your pride and your will for the great plan He has for you.

Through Him, you'll find a divine plan for your life, peace, healed relationships *and* His wisdom that'll help you overcome all that rolls your way.

Genesis 15:1
"I am your very great reward."

When God tests you, He means to perfect you and to bless you *more abundantly*. Here's a question: Can God trust you with more? And how do you handle the tests you've been given? He's given us His power to be overcomers in every situation.

James 1:2-4
In this we develop perseverance in our character which completes and matures us lacking nothing.

Is there rebellion in your life? Look to God for the solution. In trusting Him, you'll gain and not lose.

Luke 9:23-24
If anyone would come after me, he must deny himself and take up his cross daily and follow me. For whoever wants to save his life will lose it, but whoever loses his life for Me will save it.

Having self-will can cause doubt in what God can do in your life. Surrender your will for something greater He has for you.

God is your greatest Advocate

Psalm 43:5
Why are you downcast, O my soul? Why so disturbed within me? Put your hope in God, for I will yet praise Him, my Savior and my God.

Weed out all the bad-for holiness. Pray for discernment of things in your life to not be lacking in any good thing that comes from the Lord.

Through steadfastness, there is joy by abiding in Him.

James 1:2-4
In this we develop perseverance in our character which completes and matures us lacking nothing.

Do you realize when your relationship with the Lord diminishes, everything else goes astray? Spending time with the Lord and *continually* throwing off all that hinders your relationship with your heavenly Father will bring balance.

Ezekiel 34:16
I will seek that which was lost and bring again that which was driven away and will bind up that which was broken.

Joyful Living

Joshua 24:15
As for me and my house we will serve the Lord.

God wants you to discover the ways how we can live joyfully. This chapter identifies the ways that can cause us to fall.

Psalm 32:11
Rejoice in the Lord and be glad, you righteous; Sing, all you are upright in heart!

All Powerful Lord

Philippians 4:13
I can do all things through Christ who strengthens me.

You will have an upper hand over Satan if you obey the Lord's leadings.

Nehemiah 8:10
The joy of the Lord is your strength.

God can use you where you are (spiritually and physically) for His glory and purpose in your life. Let Him use you where you are and by His life-changing power you can overcome your difficulties.

Mark 10:27b
All things are possible with God.

There is joy in obedience! Living for God produces fruit-filled living where you don't care to live accordingly to the world's ways.

Philippians 2:14-16
Do everything without complaining or arguing so that you may become blameless and pure, children of God without fault in a crooked and depraved

generation in which you shine like stars in the universe.

The Love of God

Philippians 4:19
My God shall supply all your needs according to His riches in glory by Christ Jesus.

Giving glory and honor to God *in all things* is the key for joyous living. Follow His leadings especially in the small as well as the big matters, because it will make a difference in your day.

By using your talents, the Lord will bless someone through you. And by casting all your cares on Him, the Lord will be enabled to use you.

II Corinthians 12:9
My grace is sufficient for you, for My power is made perfect in weakness.

Trust God to handle your grievances by praying for those who've done wrong to you. It was God's will (surprisingly) to place you in that person's life. God didn't place you there to be defeated; His glory to be made known in your life *is* His purpose.

Pray *fervently* for His will in relationships, money situations, and trials of any kind that's been placed in your life.

Romans 8:28
And we know that in all things God works for the

good of those who love Him, who have been called according to His purpose.

No matter what the sorrow is, there's joy to come through steadfastness.

Hebrews 12:2
Let us fix our eyes on Jesus, the author and perfecter of our faith who for the joy set before Him endured the cross, scorning its shame and sat down at the right hand of the throne of God.

Our Savior-God of Love

Psalm 16:11
In Your presence is fullness of joy.

In His presence, you can get the tasks done that He's appointed you to do. He will give you wisdom for every situation. In Him, you'll find steadfastness, insight, joy and the ability to overcome the problems.
Living by the Spirit will achieve the task God's given to you into a perfect masterpiece.

Do not allow vile things to manifest within you. Run from it! Live out His life-giving principles and you will experience God's favor.

Galatians 5:25
Since we live by the Spirit, let us keep in step with the Spirit.

Fullness of joy can be found in allowing God to have first place over your circumstances and sacrificing your flesh *(worries and frustration) for His glory *and* purpose in your life. You will not be disappointed.

Galatians 5:16
*So, I say, live by the Spirit, and you will not gratify the desires of the sinful nature.

Romans 12:2

Do not conform any longer to the pattern of this world, but be transformed by the renewing of your mind. Then you will be able to test and approve what God's will is-His good, pleasing and perfect will.

He's given us His word to live more abundantly.
Joyful living includes lending a helping hand and it'll be given back in the same measure. Praying without ceasing reaps a better day *through* His wisdom He gives to you; seek Him always and you'll find Him.

And worship God for who He is, for you'll find His delight that He has for you.

Romans 15:13

May the God of hope fill you with all joy and peace as you trust in Him.

I Chronicles 16:26-27

For all the gods of the nations are idols, but the Lord made the heavens. Splendor and majesty are before Him; strength and joy in His dwelling place.

Put away your idols for a fulfilling life with Christ. You'll find a life that's free from bondage of sin and a God-driven plan for your life.

Titus 3:3-5

At one time, we too were foolish, disobedient, deceived and enslaved by all kinds of passions, and pleasures. We lived in malice and envy, being hated and hating one another. But when the kindness and love of God our Savior appeared, He saved us not because of righteous things we had done, but because of His mercy. He saved us through the washing of rebirth and renewal by the Holy Spirit.

The Glory of Steadfastness

Ezekiel 34:12

As a shepherd looks after his scattered flock when he is with them, so will I look after my sheep. I will rescue them from all the places where they were scattered on a day of clouds and darkness.

All of us time after time need guidance to walk more closely with the Lord. Here in this chapter it identifies the problems that keep us from walking in a deeper relationship with the Lord. You'll learn that He is Lord over all.

I Samuel 12:24

But be sure to fear the Lord and serve Him faithfully with all your heart; consider what great things He has done for you.

He's our constant life line

Jeremiah 29:11
"For I know the plans I have for you," declares the Lord, "plans to prosper you and not to harm you, plans to give you hope and a future."

Praise God regardless of your circumstances. Jesus is always the same. He will do for you what He has done before.

Psalm 119:105
Your word is a lamp to my feet and a light for my path.

He's sovereign over all situations in your life. Remain steadfast in your walk as I have seen His faithfulness every time in my walk.

Do not lean on your own understanding; seek *His word* for insight.

Romans 12:9
Cling to what is good.

If it's hard to choose between doing God's way or your way, remember you'll be blessed by doing it God's way.

Psalm 16:11
You have made known to me the path of life; you

will fill me with joy in your presence, with eternal pleasures of your right hand.

Praise the Lord when He gives instruction because there's a *purpose* in every one of them. It gives life to those who need it.

Psalm 16:7
I will bless the Lord who has given me counsel; My heart also instructs me in the night seasons.

He's Lord over your everyday matters

Ecclesiastes 3:1
There's a time for everything and a season for every activity under heaven.

No matter where you are today, He's given you a place there for something good.

In Him, there is power to overcome all of the difficulties that may be emotional, mental, spiritual, and physical. Having faith in God *without ceasing* will defeat the enemy for God has something good in store for you.

Numbers 24:21
Your dwelling place is secure; your nest is set in a rock.

In the hard times, God is there and His power takes precedence over the enemy.

Psalm 5:12
For surely, O Lord, you bless the righteous; you surround them with your favor as with a shield.

Renewal of your mind is standing on the promises of God. Don't let your old ways and thoughts interfere with God's new blessings for you. We are victors in Christ!

Psalm 119:44-45

I will always obey Your law, forever and ever. I will walk about in freedom, for I have sought out Your precepts.

God's everlasting gift-Grace

Matthew 7:13-14
Enter through the narrow gate. For wide is the gate and broad is the road that leads to destruction, and many enter through it. But small is the gate and narrow the road that leads to life.

Do you follow the world's ways or the Lord's? Blessings will come for those who obey Jesus. Those who will live by His Word will not waver when the storms hit, for their foundation is on Jesus Christ. God's Word is powerful enough to withstand all the storms in one's life. There's nothing lost that you cannot find in Jesus.

Forgiveness cleans you out completely. It gives joy, love, vigor for life, oneness with God, plus a clear conscience. God gives you the love and power to overcome the obstacles. There's nothing you and the Holy Spirit can't overcome.

John 15:12
My command is this: Love each other as I have loved you.

Busyness can keep you from listening to God for wisdom and direction, needed to be an overcomer.

John 6:27
Do not work for food that spoils, but for food that endures to eternal life, which the Son of Man will give you.

Mixing your old ways with the new doesn't produce life giving results.

Luke 5:38
New wine must be poured into new wineskins.

Come see that the Lord is good

I Corinthians 10:13
No temptation has seized you except what is common to man. And God is faithful; He will not let you be tempted beyond what you can bear. But when you are tempted, He will also provide a way out so that you can stand up under it.

You never have to worry about Him leaving you-He's always by your side and is *always* faithful. As He has taken me on different avenues, I've learned not to lean on my own understanding. He's trusting and all-knowing of where I'm at. He's given me wisdom concerning His purpose of why I'm there. You also can learn from Him why you're there, including the circumstances in your life. He's a good and everlasting Father who loves you entirely, and will never leave you.

Matthew 5:6
Blessed are those who hunger and thirst for righteousness, for they will be filled.

Wait for His guidance that He richly delivers. Seek Him in the morning and throughout the day so that the devil will find no place.

Lamentations 3:24
The Lord is my portion; therefore I will wait for Him.

The basis for this verse is His never-ending love for you. When you're in question, rely on Him to refute doubt because He never changes. And nothing is too big for Him to handle; He is the answer to your anger.

Peace will be given to a great measure in your home when you live by this.

God is the missing piece

Matthew 5:8
Blessed are the pure in heart, for they will see God.

To keep yourself in check, ask for sensitivity to His leadings when something isn't right. Then you'll have peace in obeying.

I John 4:19
We love because He first loved us.

Is there someone who is hard to love? Look to God, not to the problem for direction and insight. Obeying Him and His precepts will give you a long, happy life.

Mark 4:24
"With the measure you use, it will be measured to you-and even more."

God is a great God, indeed, who forgives our sins, and through His power we can forgive those who've done wrong to us. He provides such a rich inheritance for those who choose the high way of forgiveness.

I John 4:17
In this way, love is made complete in us.

Jesus is always your best Friend

I Corinthians 10:31
Whatever you do, do it all for the glory of God.

By being in tune with God, I know what God's best is for me.
The physical body is actually the Lord's temple. By feeding it well and respecting it in other ways, my relationship with the Lord has been enriched because I feel energized mentally and physically. I do it for the Lord completely. And I invite you to find the same for yourself.

I Corinthians 6:20
For ye are bought with a price: therefore glorify God in your body and in your Spirit, which are God's.

Hebrews 13:8
Jesus is the same yesterday and today and forever.

Don't be side-tracked by discouragement.
Meditate on God's Holy Word for direction. His words are life-giving, honest and pure so follow Him (Philippians 4:8). All that you need can be found in Him.
Now praise Him for all that He is and all that He's done in your life and think on these things.

James 1:22
Be ye doers of the word, and not hearers only.

When you are mocked and laughed at for doing God's will, it's their loss but your gain for doing it. You receive a renewed relationship with the Lord who sticks closer than a brother (Proverbs 18:24).

Continue to use your gifts daily for the glory of the Lord who has life-giving principles.

Matthew 5:10

Blessed are those who are persecuted because of righteousness, for theirs is the kingdom of heaven.

My friend, I'll always be faithful to you no matter what

Lamentations 3:22-23
Because of the Lord's great love we are not consumed, for His compassions never fail. They are new every morning; great is Your faithfulness.

If you get weary in certain times, rest in the Lord. Choose to lean on Him and walk in the plan He has to enrich your life.

Joshua 1:7-8
Be careful to obey all the law that was given to you; do not turn from it to the right or to the left, that you may be successful wherever you go. Do not let this Book of the Law depart from your mouth; meditate on it day and night, so that you may be careful to do everything written in it. Then you will be prosperous and successful.

Through Jesus, we can persevere. Nothing else can compare to His faithfulness. Rejoice that you have the One who is all-knowing, all-powerful, and ever-present to rely on.

Mark 10:27b
All things are possible with God.

Hebrews 11:6

And without faith it is impossible to please God, because anyone who comes to Him must believe that He exists and that He rewards those who earnestly seek Him.

Trust His word-you're special to Him

Philippians 4:19
My God shall supply all your needs according to His riches in glory by Christ Jesus.

Do you feel like an old, run down car sometimes? Let God fill you up. Here's what you do: Do no let sin get a handle on you. Repent immediately and turn away from the sin so that it won't have a stronghold on you.

Also spend time with Him. He'll fill you up mentally, physically and spiritually so you'll be ready to tackle anything. He's the One you can rely on for peace.

Romans 6:12, 14
Therefore do not let sin reign in your mortal body so that you won't obey its evil desires.
For sin shall not be your master because you are not under law, but under grace.

When you spend time with the Lord, He will provide the time to do other things.

Proverbs 3:5-6
Trust in the Lord with all your heart and lean not on your understanding; in all your ways acknowledge Him and He will make your paths straight.

Your level of trust can be measured through your patience. He is a good Father whose wisdom you can lean on for His *divine* plan for your life. Forfeit your will for the goodness of His plan. It's worth it. God is sovereign over all.

> Jeremiah 29:11
> *"For I know the plans I have for you," declares the Lord, "plans to prosper you and not to harm you, plans to give you hope and a future."*

Counselor

Romans 11:33-34, 36
Oh, the depth of the riches of the wisdom and knowledge of God! Who has known the mind of the Lord? Or who has been His counselor? For from Him and through Him and to Him are all things. To Him be the glory forever!

When you cannot avoid evil in any given place such as the workplace, your neighbors, or any other place, you can overcome it according to God's Word through prayer.

Romans 12:21
Do not be overcome by evil, but overcome evil with good.

Love Made Complete

Luke 12:6
Are not 5 sparrows sold for 2 pennies? Yet not one of them is forgotten by God. Indeed, the very hairs of your head are all numbered. Don't be afraid; you are worth more than many sparrows.

The overview of this chapter is the love He has for us and therefore completes us so that we'll be able to love others completely. Read on and see why Jesus *generously* gives.

I Corinthians 12:26
If one part suffers, every part suffers with it; if one part is honored, every part rejoices with it.

The Treasures of God

I Corinthians 2:9
"No eye has seen, no ear has heard, no mind has conceived what God has prepared for those who love Him."

Obeying God in the little things will cause you to completely love and trust Him more in the bigger things. His love can overcome all that is intended for evil. He sticks closer than a brother.

I Corinthians 10:13
No temptation has seized you except what is common to man. And God is faithful; He will not let you be tempted beyond what you can bear. But when you are tempted, He will also provide a way out so that you can stand up under it.

When you obey the Lord, it opens up the door to many blessings!

When you do not do things for others, you're spiritually shortchanging yourself.

Proverbs 28:27
He who gives to the poor will lack nothing.

Will you still love God when things don't go your way? Will

you still love Him if you don't feel good about yourself? He's still there with you. Through His strength you can master every opposition.

II Corinthians 12:9
My grace is sufficient for you, for my power is made perfect in weakness.

What talent has He given you? Give to the Lord by using your gifts and your time He's bestowed on you. In return, you'll receive a bountiful harvest of God's blessings.

Matthew 25:14
The man who had received the five talents went at once and put his money to work and gained five more.

He's always working on your behalf

Mark 10:45
For even the Son of Man did not come to be served, but to serve and to give His life as a ransom.

If you're lonely, commune with God by obeying Him. God's purpose is to draw you closer to Him. He loves you unconditionally.

John 1:7
But if we walk in the light, as He is in the light, we have fellowship with one another and the blood of Jesus, His son, purifies us from all sin.

Do you have a hard time accepting gifts and other acts of kindness from other people? If you do, you're rejecting God's provision for you. When someone does something nice for you, graciously accept it.

John 1:10-11
He was in the world, and though the world was made through Him, the world did not recognize Him. He came to that which was His own, but His own did not receive Him.

For peace in the home, honor and love God first. He knows the matters that are important, and He will give you guidance and the strength to live out your responsibilities;

He rewards those who are faithful. He is the Creator of all people, and knows how we can live peaceably.

> I Corinthians 15:58
> *Therefore, my dear brothers, stand firm. Let nothing move you. Always give yourselves fully to the Lord because you know that your labor in the Lord is not in vain.*

Invitation to Life

Matthew 6:19-21
Do not store up for yourselves treasures on earth, where moth and rust destroy, and where thieves break in and steal. But store up for yourselves treasures in heaven, where moth and rust do not destroy, and where thieves do not break in and steal. For where your treasure is, there your heart will be also.

All of the earthly desires do not have a fulfilling effect on a person's soul. Jesus came as the bread of life for *everyone* to have what we all need, and the living water that never runs dry. He knows our every intimate need. Jesus is the provider…He's the lover of our soul!

John 10:10
The thief comes only to steal and kill and destroy; I have come that they may have life, and have it to the full.

The love Christ has for us is so great. There is not one person who isn't loved by Him. His love for you is eternal, purifying and enriching. There is not a day that goes by without His hand guiding the way. His hand protects and does not harm. He gives rest and peace for all; situations for Him are not hard to handle.

Joshua 4:24
He did this so that all the peoples of the earth might

know that the hand of the Lord is powerful and so that you might always fear the Lord your God.

God of Insight

Proverbs 3:13
Happy is the man who finds wisdom, and the man who gains understanding.

Be a blessing to that person who may be unkind to you. The Lord sees a good heart and rewards the faithful.

Romans 12:21
Do not be overcome by evil, but overcome evil with good.

Have you been betrayed or embarrassed by someone? Here's what you do: Pray for that person, and be a blessing to him/her. Do you say that's not possible? God has ways that are creative because He knows that person. Handling it your way does not give room for yourself to grow. When you obey the Lord, sin will not overcome you and you'll be more than a conqueror in Christ Jesus!

Proverbs 25:21-22
If your enemy is hungry, give him bread to eat; and if he is thirsty, give him water to drink; for so you will heap coals of fire on his head, and the Lord will reward you.

Don't limit the love that you can give.

I John 2:10

Whoever who loves his brother lives in the light, and there is nothing in him to make him stumble.

He's our Perfector

Romans 13:14
Clothe yourselves with the Lord Jesus Christ, and do not think about how to gratify the desires of the sinful nature.

How well do you get along with others? It can clearly show how well your relationship is with your heavenly Father. If you notice any wrong (impatience, weariness, pride) in your actions towards others, let God have His rightful place to be cleansed.

Luke 11:9
Ask and it will be given to you; seek and you will find; knock and the door will be opened to you.

Your soul is actually yearning for God Who is steadfast and eternal. He yearns to have a relationship with you.

Are you angry at someone for doing something wrong? Change things around by not blaming them for what was done even if they are to blame. That will take your burden away and will enable you to love more like Christ. You'll be richly blessed through having a relationship with Jesus. All things matter to Him.

Hebrews 12:14

Make every effort to live in peace with all men and to be holy; without holiness no one will see the Lord.

The words of a prideful person weren't meant to defeat you-God can use it as a means to perfect you and to strengthen your faith in God.

Romans 8:28

And we know that in all things God works for the good of those who love Him, who have been called according to His purpose.

Cast All Your Cares

Isaiah 64:8
Yet, O Lord, you are our Father. We are the clay, you are the Potter; we are all the work of your Hand.

This is about finding rest in God in all of your matters. He has made us more than conquerors in His Name, and I can testify of His faithfulness in my life in so many ways. He had my life planned from the very beginning as He's done for you also. There is nothing to worry about because all things work together for His good. Seek Him in everything and you'll find rest.

Psalm 77:12
I will meditate on all your works and consider all your mighty deeds.

Let nothing else take His rightful place

You can have deliverance through salvation. God can do many things in your life. Receive Jesus Christ as your personal Lord and Savior. He is the Prince of Peace. He *alone* can conquer all things. He's been faithful in my life as my Lord and Savior and He can do the same for you. He won't disappoint you.

Hebrews 13:8
Jesus is the same yesterday and today and forever.

Cast all the anxiety you may have through spending time with God. He's the only One who can take that away.
He has a wonderful plan for your life.

I Peter 5:6-7
Humble yourselves, therefore, under God's mighty Hand, that He may lift you up in due time. Cast all your anxiety on Him because He cares for you.

Because the Lord is perfect and sufficient in all His ways, we can live victoriously!

Is there any worry in your life? He allows things to happen for a good purpose; just cast all your cares and worry upon Him for *His* good and wonderful purpose. The blessings that follow are God's goodness and more of a mature faith in the

Lord. Be glad that we're not in control.

John 15:5-6
I am the vine; you are the branches. If a man remains in Me and I in him, he will bear much fruit; apart from Me you can do nothing. If anyone does not remain in Me, he is like a branch that is thrown away and withers; such branches are picked up, thrown into the fire and burned.

The Lord is sufficient in all His ways

Hebrews 11:6
And without faith it is impossible to please God, because anyone who comes to Him must believe that He exists and that He rewards those who earnestly seek Him.

God's Word has been written for you to be an anchor when the storms hit. But you have to believe it and meditate on it for it to take hold within you so that you will not waver. He gives wisdom for you to see the light in every circumstance you have. He's the light to follow, and He will never leave you.

John 14:27-28
But the counselor, the Holy Spirit whom the Father will send in My name, will teach you all things and will remind you of everything I have said to you. Peace I leave with you; My peace I give you. I do not give to you as the world gives. Do not let your hearts be troubled and do not be afraid.

Have some quiet time with the Lord, your Savior, on a daily basis. For it's the peace of God that restores the hungry soul. His commandment to have no other gods before Me (Exodus 20:3) is meant to give Him rightful place by which we can be cleansed.

Peace with God-you will find it by giving to Him *all* your cares.

For times of impatience, seek the Lord for His all-knowingness. He gives wisdom that gives strength and light to see at the end of the tunnel. Rely on His strength continually.

Romans 8:28
And we know that in all things God works for the good of those who love Him, who have been called according to His purpose.

Nothing is too difficult for Him

Isaiah 40:31
But those who hope in the Lord will renew their strength. They will soar on wings like eagles; they will run and not grow weary, they will walk and not be faint.

Have you been caught in a bad spot where you know you don't belong? This can relate to a bad attitude or maybe you've done something that wasn't the best thing to do-perhaps you've done several things. Cast your concerns on Him. God is our guiding light; follow Him for His deliverance. He will forgive you and take you as you are. The yoke of Jesus is light, so follow Him because He is good.

Place all of you *trust* in God, not in man, and see all your insecurities go away. He's always working on your behalf. His love for you never falls short regardless of your shortcomings.

Luke 11:9
Ask and it will be given to you; seek and you will find; knock and the door will be opened to you.

Concerning a bad habit, pray to God whose power wards off all evil. As you proclaim His power, it will weaken and break.

Romans 8:37

In all these things we are more than conquerors through Him who loved us.

God's reviving gift-Grace

I Corinthians 15:58
Therefore, my dear brothers, stand firm. Let nothing move you. Always give yourselves fully to the Lord because you know that your labor in the Lord is not in vain.

Do you carry the pressures of every day on your shoulders? Do you know why God appointed these tasks for you to do? He rewards those who are hardworking and have a good attitude, not finding fault with others even if they are to blame, and loving others unconditionally. By doing this, it will keep you in God's path.

Matthew 25:14
The man who had received the five talents went at once and put his money to work and gained five more.

Do you have a hard time keeping your sight on the Lord when you encounter problems?
Rely on Him continually for a godly perspective on things.

Psalms 119:105
Your word is a lamp to my feet and a light for my path.

All things bow down to His Name

Isaiah 40:4
Every valley shall be raised up, every mountain and hill made low; the rough ground shall become level, the rugged places a plain.

What things are you facing today as mountains? When you place your trust in God *and* His will for your life, you'll realize how He uses those mountains for His glory in your life.

James 1:2-4
In this we develop perseverance in our character which completes and matures us lacking nothing.

Faith is far greater in worth than anything else in this world that we can have. Through faith, we develop a rich, satisfying relationship with our heavenly Father. Nobody else can give what the Lord provides.

He sets the captives free who live in bondage. He gives freedom so take captive every thought; throw out *all* that doesn't come from God. His Word uplifts and gives guidance because He has a plan for your life. He loves you.

Matthew 11:29
Take my yoke upon you and learn from Me for I am gentle and humble in heart, and you'll find rest for your souls.

Look no more-He's here for you.

What strongholds are in your life? Jesus is Lord over all the problems in your life. There is not one problem that He can't overthrow whether it's an addiction, depression, fear, failures, anger or even a lack of faith in God. He alone stands over all things. You can claim freedom in the name of Jesus.

Matthew 21:21-22

Jesus replied, "I tell you the truth, if you have faith and do not doubt, not only can you do what was done to the fig tree, but also you can say to this mountain, 'Go, throw yourself into the sea,' and it will be done. If you believe, you will receive whatever you ask for in prayer."

What the Cross can do for You

Luke 12:6
Are not 5 sparrows sold for 2 pennies? Yet not one of them is forgotten by God. Indeed, the very hairs of your head are all numbered. Don't be afraid; you are worth more than many sparrows.

He chose to die on the cross for your sins even if you were the only one alive. He chose to give life to you and eternal life you can have with Him if you ask Him into your heart. He has overcome the world for us to be free from bondage (John 16:33). Seek Him because the power of the cross is there for your everyday life. Read on and see what God has done.

Mark 10:45
For even the Son of Man did not come to be served, but to serve and to give His life as a ransom for many.

God's Great Love

Jesus had a big heart that didn't falter when He was crucified for our sins. What a great measurement of His love He has for us! There is not a sin too great, nor too many that the cross didn't cover and it's for everyone who asks for forgiveness. Righteousness can be yours today.

> Isaiah 53:5
> *But He was pierced for our transgressions, He was crushed for our iniquities; the punishment that brought us peace was upon Him, and by His wounds we are healed.*

What sin might you have that you can't break the chains off of you? For some it may be anger, anxiety or an addiction; anything that runs your life. Ask for discernment of things in your life that controls you.

Because of Jesus' resurrection, we are no longer under sin's control! You can have freedom through Jesus Christ.

> Galatians 5:24-25
> *Those who belong to Christ Jesus have crucified the sinful nature with its passions and desires. Since we live by the Spirit, let us keep in step with the Spirit.*

Since Jesus *chose* to die on the cross for our sins, He wants to help you with everything in your life. He wants to help you in your financial matters, your home and job life, your school work, your parenting and relationships. He even wants to give rest for your weary soul. You will find a healthy balance in your life with Jesus if you surrender all to Him.

His rewarding presence

Psalm 23:1-3, 6
The Lord is my shepherd, I shall not be in want. He makes me lie down in green pastures, He leads me beside quiet waters, He restores my soul. He guides me in paths of righteousness for His name's sake. Surely goodness and love will follow me all the days of my life, and I will dwell in the house of the Lord forever.

Because He lives, Jesus intercedes for us daily in our lives. If you haven't received Him as your Lord and Savior, ask Him today to come into your heart and ask Him to forgive all your sins. You'll live forever with Him in heaven. He'll never forget you.

John 10:9
I am the door. If anyone enters by Me, he will be saved.

Asking for forgiveness of your wrong conforms and molds you to be more like Christ making you a joyous and a better person. Receive Him today.

John 3:30
He must become greater; I must become less.

Invite the Savior into your home

John 14:6
I am the way, the truth, and the life. No one comes to the Father except through Me.

You can receive forgiveness only through Jesus Christ. He's waiting by your side who sticks closer than a brother. We have been reconciled to God through the cross of Jesus.

II Corinthians 5:20-21
We implore you on Christ's behalf: Be reconciled to God. God made Him who had no sin to be sin for us, so that in Him we might become the righteousness of God.

When you're in need, call out His name. He satisfies the hungry-who else is better that can meet your needs? He steadfastly stands by your side.

Psalm 18:30-31
As for God, His way is perfect; the Word of the Lord is flawless. He's a shield for all who take refuge in Him. For who is God besides the Lord? And who is the Rock except our God?

All things in your life are meant to glorify Him. Do not fear anything because He is with you. There's nothing that can separate you from Him. He gives light to the situation you're in-so follow Him. Then you'll find no reason to fear it at all. There's a reason why you're alive.

> John 8:31
> *If you hold to my teaching you are really my disciples. Then you will know the truth, and the truth will set you free.*

There are reasons for *all* the oppositions in your life. For His perfect will to be done, sometimes, He allows certain things to happen and not only that, it's a means to perfect you and to strengthen your relationship with your heavenly Father.

He's the One to complete you

Psalm 32:11
Rejoice in the Lord and be glad, you righteous; sing, all you who are upright in heart.

When God is for me, who can be against me? The pain you have from your past can be overcome only through the power of God. Regardless of your past, He can use you and turn your life into a masterpiece. A new life in Christ can be yours today when you ask and receive Him wholeheartedly.

Ephesians 5:1-2
Be imitators of God, therefore, as dearly loved children and live a life of love, just as Christ loved us and gave Himself up for us as a fragrant offering and sacrifice to God.

Do you need healing of a relationship gone bad? You can receive restoration by dwelling in the Holy Spirit. He'll direct your paths for a restored relationship with Him and with the other person.

John 14:26-27
The Counselor, the Holy Spirit, whom the Father will send in my Name, will teach you all things and will remind you of everything I have said to you. Peace I leave with you; My peace I give you. I do not give to you as the world gives. Do not let your hearts be troubled and do not be afraid.

New life with God

Isaiah 40:5
The glory of the Lord will be revealed, and all mankind together will see it.

Do you need healing of emotional hurts? He is Lord over all those things. You will receive healing when you seek the Lord. He restores all that is lost; He's the One to fill all your desires and needs. Look to no one else to complete you.

Mark 11:25
And when you stand praying, if you hold anything against anyone, forgive them so that you Father in heaven may forgive your sins.

John 10:9
I am the door. If anyone enters by Me, he will be saved, and will go in and out and find pasture.

What healing do you need? Whatever it may be, the Lord can heal you of your diseases, sicknesses, and weaknesses. It does not matter what it is-the Lord's Scripture says to ask and it'll be given to you (Luke 11:9).

All that you need is faith just the size of a mustard seed (Matthew 17:20). I can testify that all things are possible with the Lord. When I was young, I was diagnosed with a learning disability-some things were hard for me to grasp and understand. I didn't want to live with it. I sought out the Lord and believed Who He is and what He could do. I rejoice and say that I've been delivered from the disability completely. I have such great joy in doing the things that were once hard for me. The Lord gave me a revelation: No matter what your problem may be, He allowed it for a purpose, and He can give you deliverance! Seek Him continually for the purpose He has for your life and receive your healing. Then stand on the promises of God.

> Galatians 3:5-6
> *Does God give you His Spirit and work miracles among you because you observe the law or because you believe what you heard?*
> *Consider Abraham: "He believed God, and it was credited to him as righteousness."*

All things are possible with the Lord for those who trust in Him (Mark 9:23). You'll find peace in His divine plan. The Lord is the Great Physician.

> Romans 8:25
> *But if we hope for we do not have, we will wait for it patiently.*

Meditate on God's good word for an abundance of healing. It may take time, but don't let that defeat you. God is on your side; His Scriptures have life-changing power. Praise God, for He is Lord over all things in your life.

Proverbs 4:22
For they are life to those who find them, and health to all their flesh.

He's our only Hope

Philippians 2:9-11
Therefore God exalted Him to the highest place and gave Him the name that is above every name, that at the name of Jesus every knee shall bow in heaven and on earth and under the earth and every tongue confess that Jesus Christ is Lord to the glory of God the Father.

When you encounter an obstacle to your faith, it's not the end of a healing. Jesus is there waiting for you to come to Him. Seek Him with all your heart, mind, and soul to be made whole.

John 10:10
The thief comes only to steal, kill and destroy; I have come that they may have life, and have it to the full.

Your healing is secure because God placed the desire in your heart in the first place.

Romans 5:3-5
We also rejoice in our sufferings because we know that suffering produces perseverance; perseverance, character; character, hope. And hope does not disappoint us because God has poured out His love into our hearts by the Holy Spirit, whom He has given us.

In every trial, pray steadfastly accordingly to God's will to possess God-bearing fruit.

James 5:16

The prayer of a righteous man is powerful and effective.

Hearing God's Voice

Luke 5:38
New wine must be poured into new wineskins.

In this chapter, it talks about the richness of having a relationship with the heavenly Father leading you to a life of purpose and intimacy with the Lord. It also identifies the sources that interfere hearing Him.

Matthew 7:13-14
Enter through the narrow gate. For wide is the gate and broad is the road that leads to destruction, and many enter through it. But small is the gate and narrow the road that leads to life.

Rewarding life with God

Galatians 5:22
But the fruit of the Spirit is love, joy, peace, patience, kindness, goodness, faithfulness, gentleness and self-control.

Throughout the day, God speaks in a still, quiet voice. His word speaks in peace, not in anger towards you, leading you in righteousness.

John 7:38
He who believes in Me, as the Scripture has said, out of his heart will flow rivers of living water.

When you do not answer the Lord when He knocks, you reject His power in all other areas of your life.

John 10:10
The thief comes only to steal and kill and destroy; I have come that they may have life, and have it to the full.

You will not be lacking any good thing when you respond-He's waiting patiently for you to answer Him regardless of how you've been.

Psalm 19:7
The law of the Lord is perfect, reviving the soul. The statutes of the Lord are trustworthy, making wise the simple.

Psalm 16:7
I will praise the Lord who counsels me; even at night my heart instructs me.

Spiritual cleanliness with the Lord helps you hear His voice, which you can have through *receiving* forgiveness, being obedient, and even fellowshipping with Him throughout the day. Last but not least, ask for sensitivity.

Proverbs 4:13
Hold on to instruction, do not let it go; guard it well, for it is your life.

His Word is the Wellspring of Life

Psalm 63:3
Your lovingkindness is better than life.

One obstacle that keeps you from listening to God is when you're upset. Reach out to Him and tell Him what's on your mind-He understands. He has the solution to every concern you have.

Joshua 24:15
But as for me and my household, we will serve the Lord.

Are you lacking direction? Heed to the Lord's leadings because you'll find that nobody else can fulfill your needs. Seek His rewarding guidance He has for you.

Matthew 18:12-14
If a man owns a hundred sheep, and one of them wanders away, will he not leave the ninety-nine on the hills and go to look for the one that wandered off? And if he finds it, I tell you the truth, he is happier about that one sheep than about the ninety-nine that did not wander off. In the same way your Father in heaven is not willing that any of these little ones should be lost.

Do you have a hard time sleeping at night? Use that time to spend with the Lord.

Colossians 4:2
Devote yourselves to prayer, being watchful and thankful.

You are a Gift from God

Isaiah 64:8
Yet, O Lord, you are our Father. We are the clay, you are the Potter; we are all the work of your Hand.

To have God's will for your life, you must surrender yours. It doesn't matter if you're a failure; He can use you. If you grew up feeling no one liked you; you're found worthy to God. I personally realized that He can take those things and turn them *all* around for His good. Remember to surrender your will (all of your concerns, hurts and your anger) for the goodness of His plan. Lean on Him because He loves you and will deliver you if you seek Him with all your heart, mind and soul. He promises not to leave you.

John 15:5-6
I am the vine; you are the branches. If a man remains in Me and I in him, he will bear much fruit; apart from Me you can do nothing. If anyone does not remain in Me, he is like a branch that is thrown away and withers; such branches are picked up, thrown into the fire and burned.

Do you know the calling God has for your life? To know it, seek Him earnestly with all of your heart. He can use you where you are spiritually and physically. He has granted you all the things you need to accomplish His will for your life. I heartily encourage you to find His calling for your life-and by no means is your purpose mediocre.

Jeremiah 29:11

"For I know the plans I have for you," declares the Lord, "plans to prosper you and not to harm you, plans to give you hope and a future."

It's Wonderful to Obey

II Corinthians 10:5
Casting down arguments and every high thing that exalts itself against the knowledge of God, bringing every thought into captivity to the obedience of Christ.

The revelations God spoke to you are seeds to sow within you to reap the blessings. Reject the deceiver's words- it the words of Christ that have life!

Having no pride in yourself can release the blessings of God on your life. Without that interfering, you're receptive to the Lord's calling on your life. Without Him you can do nothing (John 3:27).

Ask the Lord to identify any pride you may have, for in return, you'll receive an abundance of His power and His purpose for your life.

I Corinthians 2:9
"No eye has seen, no ear has heard, no mind has conceived what God has prepared for those who love Him."

When you listen to God's voice throughout the day, you'll find joy and contentment. Through obedience He rewards you, and not only that, His divine plan is being unfolded.

Remember, He knitted you in your mother's womb, with a purpose for your life. Seek Him with all your heart even when it's hard, and you will not be lacking in any good thing.

Psalms 139:13-14
For You created my inmost being: You knit me together in my mother's womb. I praise You because I am fearfully and wonderfully made; Your works are wonderful, I know that full well.

Printed in the United States
67465LVS00002B/21